Free Verse Editions
Edited by Jon Thompson

& in Open, Marvel

Felicia Zamora

Parlor Press
Anderson, South Carolina
www.parlorpress.com

Parlor Press LLC, Anderson, South Carolina, 29621

Printed in the United States of America
S A N: 2 5 4 - 8 8 7 9

Library of Congress Cataloging-in-Publication Data on File

978-1-60235-984-0 (paperback)
978-1-60235-985-7 (pdf)
978-1-60235-986-4 (epub)
978-1-60235-987-1 (ibook)
978-1-60235-988-8 (mobi)

1 2 3 4 5

Cover design by David Blakesley.
Cover image: "Flurry of Wings: Clustered" by Jessica Owings
    Crouch. Used by permission
Printed on acid-free paper.

Parlor Press, LLC is an independent publisher of scholarly and
trade titles in print and multimedia formats. This book is available
in paperback and ebook formats from Parlor Press on the World
Wide Web at http://www.parlorpress.com or through online and
brick-and-mortar bookstores. For submission information or to
find out about Parlor Press publications, write to Parlor Press,
3015 Brackenberry Drive, Anderson, South Carolina, 29621, or
email editor@parlorpress.com.

Contents

empty haunt; inlet *3*

A Long Road Never Takes Us *5*
At Last Summer Let Go *6*
Sacrament *7*
Caught in Diastole *9*
Before Winter *10*
Alone at the Lake *11*
A Constant Spin Resides *12*
Purpose of Dance *13*
I Hear the Blue Jay Sing *14*

dance {dance} dance *15*

Intersections *17*
Still These Lovely Works Beyond Us *18*
Brain Waves *19*
Picture of the Hive *20*
In Perihelion *21*
Broken Things *22*
Centripetal *23*
{Honest} Random {Caused by Desire
    to De-Categorize} Self *24*
Understanding Words Fail & Weave in Simultaneity *25*

imbibe {et alia} here *27*

orts: a poem *27*

Imbibe {Et Alia} Here *28*

flutter & flash   *61*

In Hush   *63*

A Lesson   *64*

Witness Here: A Limited Thing   *65*

Vernal   *66*

We Return Sparkling   *67*

Across the Blown, Inward Breeze   *68*

Toward the End of Day   *69*

Hummingbirds   *70*

Soon   *71*

Blue Jays in the Yard   *73*

Acknowledgments   75

Free Verse Editions   77

About the Author   79

For Goose,

Be sturdy & wide-eyed—open to the wonders of this world; let not a single moment close you.

Love, Aunt Felicia

There are things to be said. No doubt.
And in one way or another
they will be said. But to whom tell

the silences? With whom share them
now? For a moment the sky is
empty and then there was a bird.

> —Cid Corman,
> *from "There Are Things to Be Said"*

Here where the poem becomes
                    ladders again,
the little girl returned with candy
& a *nearly* on her lips

> —Joshua Marie Wilkinson,
> *Lug Your Careless Body Out of the Careful Dusk*

& in Open, Marvel

empty haunt; inlet

A Long Road Never Takes Us

Fish poke the surface, entice
ripples to hoard the shore, release,
hoard again. The light shifts
everything here. Bug spray in my hair,
hummingbird at the picnic table, the clouds
lulling under their transformative bellies—
there has always and never been this—
longing of a mind carried in a body
here. The sun touches my shoulder, old friends
gathering at one of the lake's many mouths
luring all senses; *caught*. The wash of waves,
sectioned and small, so persistent: the body
functioning without my consent.
I spent my *whole life* neglecting the lap
in my ears, half listening out of body
of water; drowning in my own fluid-filled spaces.
The kayaker's need of water's drift: my need
to witness. Infinite rhythms we share
and scavenge. The crows scale the Ponderosas
tip to tip—games in birds' eyes. I want to believe
a long road never takes us. We are led
with wings and tympani and slick wet
inside and out. The canoe wears its name
Old Town— red and passionate on the bank;
footprints trail away and to: abandon
casts no reflection in late summer's glow.
Five months out of winter's gait
empty will haunt this inlet again. An unknown
tune from the boy behind me. Hums still
as his grandfather baits his line; *I might know
how*, escapes him. Silence and toil. The ever sway
of small legs on a bench—reaching.

At Last Summer Let Go

The leaves in descent yellow
behind your back. Mystery
in the senses we ignore. Caught
just out of reach: the balloon,
string-less and wind swept forgets. We
open-palmed, stars paint galaxies
at the back of our pupils. Collection
until shutter. To undo the heavens
this brain harbors with guilt
cage and key in constant turn, a habitué
of adorning everything with wings.

Sacrament

Before tolls deepen the landscape,
the handshakes, the *sorry* stitching
in furrowed brows, the church settles
& you hear the steeple *sigh*. Air steps

closer to you, like a child approaches,
hesitant, question on her lips. To grow here—
a town no bigger than a thumb, you tasted
the Body & licked your teeth after wine.

What you've done & undone
for sacrament. As a child you chanted
the Nicene Creed, while you undressed
a boy across from you with fervid pupils

& tingles between your thighs. Confirmation
liturgy commensal of body & blood: faith
in the pastor's lack of telepathy. *Innocence*
laired in your temporal lobe, along with *lust*
& palms in sweat, aware of both.

You return to rows of slotted boxes;
parishioners" names: *Cleveland; Lettow; Grimes*—
small spaces of keeping. Places defined
by brood & lineage. Your fingers trail openings

& fall into hollow drum, *drum*. Your name
once aperture, an invitation; vow. Distance &
years untie the knot of place to you. Unbound
between aisles of pews, you spectator

arrive at *The Last Supper*, heavy frame in dip
offsets the scene. Your eyes swallow you
back to the kitchen table, to each stroke
of your mother's hand, outlined gently; changing

brushes; capped colors labeled *1-11*; a guided
masterpiece. Grandma Evelyn peering over shoulder;
unction in a simple squeeze, "A fine addition
to any home". *Home*: four letters burnt

into the underside of each rib; vestige
drug with us, round & round. Dizzying affair.
Are we called—how instinct of *V*
dwells in the goose? Are we called *home*

ventricles feeding heart? O, duel system
circulating us. These bells, someday
will be yours. These bells
already yours. & *home* is a small round lid

paint drying inside. & with water
so elemental, discovery & rediscovery:
carillon batons & pedals play
by ghosts & echoes of ghosts.

Caught in Diastole

Mist exhales the foothills—up and over saturates, dissipates
and lilacs and moist; twigs and pods strewn: this becoming under other

held in a gentle roll. Brontide in the lightening flash mimics
the cardiac cycle—*here again,* we caught in diastole

filling, filling, until our walls cave us, change our shape,
require we purge the hoard. The body knows forgiveness

in the senses: odorant molecules of rain carry
promises in the glomerulus; our eyes in dance. Jealous

sky gathers and gathers, dilation keeps us
longing for—*elements imbibing until…elements in fall*—breach.

Before Winter

What barren waits for. Flesh
culls a layer, a layer more. Wind becomes
estranged. The branches salvage. The Vs;

the Vs greater-than, less-than the sky
& what is gray heavies
in the lack of light, in the pupils

wanting horizon to look back, & long.
What illuminates just before dark.
What we call a season, because we must

call something up the throat, the epiglottis
vibrates above the slope of the tongue,
attached. What something

must we offer back
to the swirl, the hemispheric homeland—bound
in pirouette. Our spines knowing we are

in dance. Our minds chant stability. A feather
tufted in feathers. Before Vs, there were beaks. A singular beak
points. An instinct is a direction. You smell the flurry

before the flake. & barren is intermittent:
a season is stacked moments
melting through our mouths caught in capture.

Always a wait within a gasp. An entrance
in lips gaped apart. You taste
dried leaves on your pallet & a promise

of warmth to tend the frost, to take the low bow
where sleep peels at the inside of a thing—
say 'hibernate' here. To burrow in something other

than self. Say 'what continues to adapt.' Say 'inclement.' Stay
still in a thought; cloak a word
over the mouth spool. Understand, you will be let go.

Alone at the Lake

How often your mind mirrors the lake,
surface frozen, mid ripple.
What was once water
rips from sand at the seam—
to be unstitched; bits of you
scatter & resemble seeds
dried & un-sowable. Beyond shore
depths teem. What keeps
a body held in? Sewn breath
of January wrinkles thoughts
here—where buoys strew
float-less & sad—a crime
scene in wait of discovery.
You want to believe
a shore may stretch forever,
guarded circumference of self
looping in & around a body
immobilized; the amygdala
disobeys dormancy, streams
memory without consent.
& you say "undone" & "regret"
as part of language the cerebral cortex
muddled out of nothing
to understand, and yet—an echo
of spring unravels clues
piling in the dense clouds. & mystery
swims in each opening
of the aortic valve. To dissipate
upon notice, or not be noticed at all—
precipitation the sky kept; air
feeding lungs; gray matter
in action: words
forming within a tendril of brain
& all the world synapses; all the world
fluid & permeable—you are
hardly able. Hardly.

A Constant Spin Resides

Consider: the dim of day; the deep swallow of horizon;
horizon's gullet {your fingers stroke empty
larynx, in search of Adam's apple};
the trajectory of *never reaching*; what possibilities
of *vast* and *space* can be whittled in the brain, and let fly
through pupils; the tongue a sling shot;
the tongue a luring wave. Imagine here. {Speak
your eyes into dialect—} The flesh conduit,
not-so-subtle robe, withering dress: what hides?

A constant spin resides in all things kissed
to live. The lips? The lips remain
as capture-able as the sun peaking—then dusk.
{The lips remain…} To look at the core of the Earth
outside brainwaves and sketches of supposition:
here—here magic remains
a gullet of blind dark. *Kiss, kiss.*

Purpose of Dance

To sit in the wind and feel entered:
a porous gate: organ full: empty buzz.
Pinpoint the moment, down the throat,
where the skeletal binding fuses itself
and melody embeds in veins:
the source of motion
below the clavicle—the aortic valve
astute at work. Quaking
occurs inside us all. In other forests
aspens clap their leaves, orchestra
in the tips of branches; you in audition
ripe for stage. *Quake*:
a bell struck and stuck; the curtain
red for reaping—first
of showmanship. Do not ignore
the call set in origin, deep inside
the medulla oblongata of a thing
in dance, made only for the purpose of dance.

I Hear the Blue Jay Sing

& the clouds in their deep mourn, recede
revealing a color so opposite of January
thicker than *bleu celeste*, a tincture of
ocean washed with opal, my eyes
stuck in comprehension give bow. & melody
taps at my eardrums. The passerine bird lifts
syrinx pitches a truth so full
I sweep, terribly & gently past beak
down forked trachea to nestle
between bronchi, here I am
extant & dual-songed—in one breath,
I belong to other. In one exhalation, I perch
among the membranes, quivering.

dance {dance} dance

Intersections

& the robins *t* their wind-strewn bodies
into infinities: ovals of ovals, stretched
by their connective paths & the scent
of where wings once were. These street lights,
pillars of command and obey, become
place of witness: the side street where the parade begins,
the movement of robin's need of—you
in your car lost in this moment. The rain
distant, yet east in peripherals. Direction gathers you
damp pavement in your nostrils— the sun loving
a leaf after—these affairs
stop us. The *why* of these birds lulls
your brain in dance & now your eyes
are wings: spread open;
breast bone popping in each contortion of your spine
under & over you; palms push out
so forward fingers arch back; head against the nape
of your back in rise; chin to chest in dive: synchronicity
with limbs— the motion you long for
& the tail fanned out in front of you
disappears magically in the loop—

Still These Lovely Works Beyond Us

Down down the street, the moon props the tree-line:
a question mark's bottom, bold and spying, wonder still
caught in clouds. In this blue into blue, night creeps under
sun lugging day in its belly; dreamer's constant visitor
in witness—me. And all lines blur. And all colors bleed:
simultaneous this *awe* and *shame* in my gut. We construct
out of unfinished, half equivocal. Lines in my palm speculate
me, and I them. The seed is the answer to the cottonwood; or
first the cottonwood, or seed? In any mid-sized {any}, roundabouts
confuse. Draw an outline of your face. What have you
drawn? Language wraps like the long lick of seasons
swallow one into another. Anticipate C because of B. What if we ran
out of alphabet? I hang U on the wall; forgot U in the move. Funny,
how *ownership* fails. You belong to no one else now, moon
your own reflection in your spectacles. To describe
illusive things: your shadow in darkness, music behind walls,
origins, the heart mended, the exact digits
behind the period of pi, fall's arrival—mystery
lingers still these lovely works beyond us. Unravel
a tune before notes, one that strikes on your tongue
and summons your brain. Your shoulders sway
without your approval. We action and reaction
without the *why*, and make use of our oblivious
nature seizes us, turns our chins to the side
saying, *See...   just see.*

Brain Waves

The whisper {disjointed}
of soul promised inside: you
doubled and asymmetric: parageusia—
the tongue only tastes
tongue and mouth: no simple:
{insert *anything blabber*} here: a shadow
cast from a border collie
gnaws a leg, prefers his own
flesh: a collective: a feeding trough:
consciousness plugged {your lips form
"in"—erase; construct a "socket"}: controlled
role: who watches:
energy out of: {what cliché:
to begin} stomach knows feeding—
colligate the kitchen from there: hunger
dirties the sheets—saturates, we learned:
longing within crevasses and folds:
tendrils bunch and think
nothing of you.

Picture of the Hive

Fingers to keyboard, cyber-minded
when the photo hits your inbox—
Hexagons burnt into wood: a pattern
innately inside the bee, graffiti-ed
by human hands. *A welcome*
for whom? A home of sorts. Display
of bees; built production
of honey and love. A patch of bodies
leaks up from the lower opening
disobedient; gravity uncontained
in roil of wings and legs and thoraxes.
Vision of keeping. How insect grows
beyond singularity. Shared action
creates: a bee on a bee on a bee
becomes swarm: how one must settle
into colony, endure abdominal glands
producing wax, barbs on the stinger,
following and giving. *Does the bee*
ever feel disconnected? A moment of life
pixelated across the screen. You, now,
deep in apiology, witness yourself
on haunches inside the bee yard,
pollen and honey in your hair, swept
in the zzzzzzzzz dwelling inside you.

In Perihelion

It is the orbit that heavies me. Lagan swing:
tethers built in

cells and atoms. A sunken thing
with promise of drift. Abundance of the lack

of shores. Reciprocal to motion. *What must
sling back.* Jelly fish must obey the lap.

Egret, hunts motionless in crouch,
swivels head side-to-side to reduce refraction.

Beak a spear: caught
in cycles—inherent in design. The tongue

bound in the mouth, learns. A child's game
grew first in the thalamus; consciousness' guard.

What doesn't grow in seclusion—know
the tilt of the earth inside you; a thought specs

in the mind and announces itself. Bewitch you.
Are we not in pull to this? Crouched like egrets.

The ever-stream held tight in the wrap:
skeletal muscles, fat, and tissues. Bits becoming.

And we flow
as we must flow to cradle together
all fleshy heavens, all dowsed in sun's lull.

Broken Things

The underside of flesh {where light must soak}: a broken thing
etches —songs score along blood vessel, your throat
cannot sing the occult notes, your lungs in constant
deflate {all these wounds puncture wounds}, fill
unable–the scribe of defining {a heart
borrows what must *must* keep rhythm} unbeknownst
the brain in its bone-ivory tower; tendrils
lighthouse the salt-licked shores while tethered to spine
spirals wither in {under use, over use—*choose if you suit*} diurnal
tide-song in the belly where you first begot: a mistake
that emerged your infant hands in clutch. Before wail, before
amniotic drained from your pores, a broken thing
gave 23 chromosomes to an egg which enveloped—you
diploid and aligned {wave and inlet: lovers
raging by their attraction to sun and moon {you moon;
you moon, dark and suffocating}}: ancient
civilizations worshiped the stars
with both awe and fear they were denied—origin
lay only in a compass-less map and the bright bright
burn against the dark {galaxies streaming inside
out} forcing them to *look, look away, look again.*

Centripetal

I saw the rabbit in the drainpipe and thought *you* not *bunny*. Ode to hide
in linings; our innate desire to crease our edges and fold—origami style
into ergonomic chairs that still contort us; out of flesh into words
we missile, retract, blow ourselves up—over and over
like a child itches the bite; blood; more blood. We don't learn to suck flesh
we just do: pull the open slice right into the mouth—taste ourselves
raw fluid and ease. Pseudo-oval shape of the snake tail in the snake jaws, unable
to swallow the joke. My nephew learned to sooth on his own. I lay
next to him, listening to him knock tongue to mouth roof—symphony
in clicks of his lips *apart, together, apart.* Do we learn to mimic or mimic to learn?
I test my lips; think of Jack; smile. *Learn.* When I watch the kids, I'm "Aunt ___".
Days following, the prefix sticks and oozes—identity mess. *Oh, the rabbit*
tapes back her ears; pretends to slither among the pipes, metal and hollow. My rabbit heart.
My rabbit reflex set to *scurry, scurry.* A part of learning chunks away at us. A part
we play requires us to unlearn. *Instinct instinct instinct.* Shed of filament—thoracic cavity
exposed; I stick my fingers through ribs, poke ventricles (left/right), feel the fill
apex of the heart nestled to the diaphragm—lovers. As a system always in cycle
in recycle around {} until cut, or broken, or rigor mortis consumes. A mind
in a body grows seeded by hand or by wind spreading: a field
in a field in a field. Inside holds something, if at last: space.

{Honest} Random {Caused by Desire to De-Categorize} Self

"When all else fails…" I say to myself. When all else fails I go to the thesaurus. When I go to the thesaurus to discover religion and get sidetracked by porn, I lie about this action. I lie about this one too. Deciphering is the easy—all the rest breaks, breaks, my concentration lacks luster; bees honeycombing in my: {you want to say *bonnet, cleaver me-* no} heavy cranium. All shade in these gelatinous tendrils: shady as shady goes. {Head stroke here.} I twitch at being told what to do. {Insert term: *micromanage*. Do not insert an emoticon. I am sad I know what *emoticon* stands for.} Yoga classes – out. Pottery – out. And yet, pushback from curiosity . . . journalistic ellipsis remind me of how I tell stories. Did you hear the one about my brother and me getting kicked out of swimming lessons? Over and over again. I dream of drowning. My subconscious wastes away on fear and more fear. Over and over again I tell this story. Polite fosters energy loss. "Swimming privileges revoked…" I think I make a guttural sound. What is in me is the truth. What is in the truth is me. What the mind tells the body; what the body tells the mind; what the body tells the body. Sticky lies on lips. {I taste my own fear of drowning.} Aren't we all: synchronicity? A stream of consciousness: then there's this: what's wrong with tubing in the shallow bodies? {Very Midwestern: *tubing*.} Always, a thing held in; a thing held back. Constraints beg {disobedience} {perhaps a lullaby tuned to Lady Gaga}: eyes on this page hold contempt for the words written {"lullaby tuned to Lady Gaga"}. {No, not yours, mime.} Lack of sound {em}powers. {Say *nonverbal* here.} The mime isn't bad at her job; she's just chatty. Remember when "ga ga" was a baby's term. I don't recall *starting* from anywhere; self-help books tell me I'm lucky to be here. What does *lucky* look like? Oh, the alliterations roll now. Language: a vestige I tote under my arms, in hopes the clouds pass. Language: I burden you, then turn to you for redemption.

Understanding Words Fail & Weave in Simultaneity

Knuckle, a knock on the breastbone—
Who's there, escapes your medulla oblongata.
The bulb lights up & you, all a thrush, beat
your tiny beak, acorn grasping, against chest
to resuscitate that organ of chambers
floating inside sac: nominal to sum
parts in gather. Wall in a wall in a wall: the ghost
believes & holiness triunes. *What keeps in?*
Origins of voice: spells cast. The flesh & spirit
chew each other up; spit each other out
kneel at the *moon, moon, moon*—you epistolize
over & over & —to capture the "o" spills
your lips so willing to empty, the ribs
played upon by harpist, in torment, lull.

imbibe {et alia} here

orts: a poem

Imbibe {Et Alia} Here

These bones in the mouth
chew syllabics out
of synaptic response. Jaw clicks
molars in chant; these incisor cogs:
{the sum:} conjures
of fluid and cells, permeating.

{ }

Slur "and per se" —
a child in recitation
learns sways and rhythms.
Statement becomes
&. & how the marvel opens
mouth slings punctuation to mean.

                                        { }

What lends to the transit:
an aortic sack constructs
inside a small chest, encapsulated
in mother's amniotic sack. We all
woven into light
dark weft: the first world warps our lips.

{ }

Truant, your idle
in between things {stroke
your thing-flesh, your thing-
swallow} yawns inside itself.
Slice the oak's trunk; her belly
carved, despite stillness.

{ }

Eyes fill the aspen bark, oversee
the nest's sag—feather tucks
twig and scrap stitch—reminisce in mend;
lungs crisp in air; now who's witnessing
all statues caught {once} the sun sullies
horizon—visions unravel you.

{ }

More than twice-removed
these lips build "forest"—and your hands
strangle metal, rub the fire out of palms,
swat at the sun: jealous of the give.
Plebeian: *forge* and *design*: {distant
semblance} conjugate only in act.

{ }

Choose a side to pivot from. Any shoulder
leads to a degree. In turn, do you find yourself
in wide open grassland? Field of heather?
Row of rye? In all this open
your haunches constrict around the hip
to sit or kneel, whichever the body prepares for.

{ }

Peel back the skin of a { ____; ____}
cottonwood shoot, two rings forming—
you shall find: hidden wet; fibers
in lust to mold; a body
exposed; the soon-to-be. Sometimes, we reap
the producing dark.

{ }

Inevitability is inevitable.
Who counts the sparrows, heavy-ing limbs,
inching to the trunk during blizzard?
Who washes the runes, hiding them
in cupboards: one more plate
to eat from or forget.

{ }

When cupped, the hand
a nest harbors what it must—
see your palm {a nest}
rested inside {this nest}. Branches
now, our arms tangle {perch here}
splay the wood, a rib, un-caged.

{ }

What interiors the egg
is not what vessels the egg.
{This is not a riddle.} Elapse.
{Nor you.} A passage opens
must, must. Follow the curvature
shell: a horizon, in form.

{ }

On the topic of legerdemain
what if you cease to witness?
Clouds still roam about; dew dews; generations
of swallows share eaves. Less all this.
More concrete; more pixels; more cyber-
everything. How vatic we {de}construct.

{ }

No, the hive sags
by design. Our honeycomb
cerebellum. Our honeycomb
aortas. All buzz.
Say *apiary*. Your jaw: hive in construct.
You say *apiary*. You mean *b{ee}one yard.*

{ }

None of this comes
{insert *with a price tag* or *naturally* here}.
Intention funneled down
from the very first accident. Look
how these hands whittle, barren. Look
how this tongue scorches, lasting.

{ }

Cast {in/away} of—
the fallow only quiescent
remembers the harrow's disks
mid-slice. What remains
tethered without root
binds in haunt, in lack of.

{ }

Much said of the aching forearm
severed of wrist, curling
specter-fingers on command. Once, you
shuddered at slants and leans
of headstone rows. How barbaric
the etches; how lovely the keep.

{ }

The wheelbarrows all
toppled to sides, pissed on
with graffiti, paint re-
claimed. The skin of a thing
weathers {*despite*} storms.
Do you feel scraping {*at* or *to*}?

{ }

To dream of spiders is to dream in multiplication,
in limbs. Once an appendix worked for the body.
Once tonsils served. What remains of remains?
All the catacombs overflow with dust,
once weres—genetic traditions in decay:
arms extended, forgotten in reach.

{ }

Perceive {*yes, we*
swim in parietal lobe} the shale languid
in the palm. Beach echo. No rest
in places of birth and song. Tell the story:
cliff grooves to shape
the chip in fall, flies.

{ }

Absence winnows,
undresses the memory—until—
the photographs have leaked into the air.
What the palm holds, calculates
the worth of a thing not defined by economic
stature in the back bone—the cortexes, teeming.
{ }

She keeps fish. Docent in manner,
her eyes perch the lip of the sofa;
{witness} the Cichlid devours
the tank. A body
{of water} holds {death} unevenly,
yet fully. Her lens: a guide for dwelling.

{ }

What of the swim in waterless spaces:
back-stroke hypnotized
in air conditioning. We've lost—
what is touch other than
to seek out: remove self from self:
grin—the ambiguity— the bare.

{ }

Bribe the whalebone in your back—
aqueous, again. Calcaneus sheds
the heel: aqueous, again. Loosen the pores,
membrane thin {be fluid}: to be swam in
{what gape means} and fed from. Once a
food-chain included you.

{ }

Take stalk in—
your 37 trillion cells—roots
wilt in wait of {heaven
releases us in shower; fallen} wet {state/
act}. Hibernate in deep in lean; pray
—*liquid bone, liquid sky; yes, yes.*

{ }

All feminine, we birth
of wom{an}b—we first imbibe
liquid breath, liquid mother—
drinking her guts, we form
{motile {sperm to egg}, ossein {percent of per-
cent}}: carvings in the placenta, before passage.

{ }

When we speak of *ho{rr/n}or*
speak transparently; moon jellyfish
dances surf, inland stretches— suffocates in air
and sand. Polyp suffers what we avert from—
innate majesty in firefly abdomen, luring
palms and mason jars.

{ }

We watch, through sorrow and lenses
a lymph node swells—
{into mass, what is not random}
supplicates to *whys* and *reasons*.
In subtle strokes, madness carves
trails in brainwaves: *Going?*

{ }

Autonomic {all
stimuli desire in{*e*}ternal}—this un{bridled}-
derstanding {*think   think   think*}:
how the river undresses the shore
lines a boundary; imagine
casing you wrap you around.

{ }

You desire *here*—taste
fills your pallet. The outline of you in float,
devouring {our cords in our bellies,
cords in our spines; how we attach—
umbilical/cerebral {permeable
mouth open in fluid}} space.

{ }

Leave this distance; this observation
tunnels out onto hands; motion:
a stop in the heart waking you,
dilated pupils—*so damned*
happy to lack control. Our own flesh
bought us here. The payment, flays us.

{ }

Night undresses behind panes—
catches you. The snow globe
dizzies; a layer of white collects you
thunder heart in moiety of shadows.
Cover engulfs cover: duplicates
competing dark will take this too. *This too:*

{ }

Once the empty heavies
{   }
{   }
Crawl back to midnight: fluid and collagen-rich
{   }
Sewn up inside you, now.

{ }

flutter & flash

In Hush

Sun's lug: a blazon crown in horizon. All shadows
seeded in shadow, linger—what gape *before*
recede, *before* light reclaims. Space dances in
the in-between, diachronic of self –
luminance. Ineffable
a moment—we have been brought here: soul-
heavy, naked gait, eyes feasting. You witness:
tree trunks burnt into morning. You shift
your eyes away; the burnt follows
the grey of landscape emerges through the onyx-
brushed blue; & we enter
something elemental, something
coaxing; the dream left us here to puzzle deeper
into the dream. Hushed as a baby, we fell
in love with movement of lips, rigidity of teeth,
song forming in the back of our throat. Larynx
cajoles our hymns out, out—*release*. We find
our brain in hum; our brain translucent in early
fires of day, absorption ready. You find yourself
in stop; the crosswalk brisk; your hair sweeping
cheeks and forehead in gentle waves. *Intake*.
Intake this color rich, cold comfort—*rising*. &
the geese, in long forget, go about their honking;
the fire station opens its eyelids one at a time
in a slow, backwards wink— motion
by motion, the city wakes as part of you & you
gazer, your mouth puckered in *hush*.

A Lesson

Tar snakes the asphalt under the cold glow of the streetlamp;
Christmas bulbs radiate the cul-de-sac. From the second story window
the weighted hand of *hush* sweeps over this place; quiet builds. Envelopes
stack on the kitchen table below you; printed dates, numbers shuffle
your mind. *Breath in; breath out: a calculator of what keeps you.* Caught
in your own stare, your pupils swallow the night
behind the pane. *Choke in the throat*—when you were a child, you remember
lying down below the mulberry tree, tracing the crooked bark with your eyes,
believing you could fall straight up, walk on the bellies of crows; flight
kept you spinning. To feel the world inside out, to ball it up in your hand,
tear a piece for you, and share the rest. You arose stained
in hues of purple and violet; marked by your longing. You circumnavigated
that ball. *Tore too little? Tore too much?* The December air reveals
breath from your mouth; visibility a comfort. You find your way
to the trunk of the cottonwood. First one knee, then the other.
A lesson. Then palms. The body learns to contort, reshape, accept
new motion as *body.* On your back, branches tickle the stars
rub fast their distant warmth, *Morus rubra,* spells cast in the dark ripening
what inhabits you now—the sweet smell of drupes on your cheek.

Witness Here: A Limited Thing

You clamber from winter: frail
flesh, wounded eyes. Time's fickle
indifference seeps less in the elongated rays,
your shadow stretches away from you
how sunset never, never approaches.
The aspen buds curl tips. Everything yawns—
out of. Your porous pupils
barometers to desire the wind's warp, warm
cool of *promises*. Whispers under bark,
where tunnels make you into visions. Your name:
a ring carving in a rib—abacus
of spine. All these tuning bones; stream
of muscle. Heart: a rendered nest: *flutters; flutters*
built at center where skeletal branches keep
huddle for the robin's return—
she, unlike you, will not avail the tatters
after the thaw. You never beyond lovely limit: *here*.

Vernal

When grey defines the vittate sky. Moment just before
dormant bud scale, then shrug, then unfurl. To witness
fleets you; lips part the escaping sigh, *if only here
not there*. The wool tightly crimps to the sheep's loin; yet,
we claim burl for our eyes anyway. Numbers in count
spellbind us. In cadence, the fly enters with the dog.
We watch it roam the ceiling, traverse the cabinet door
lone and godlike. We cock our heads
at cottonwood's girth; imagine sliced, the rings etched—
latitudinal ripples frozen to pith. Our effrontery buries
our shameful brains in our shameful hearts. The robin,
her chest ablaze against the skeletal forest, *must
must forgive us.* She nests in the hollow of our skulls
and builds sapwood anew. What lofts in this cold tinder:
eggs and promise of flight. Left in gape, we stammer
in the sun's pale face; loosen our scarves; toe the dirt;
lick our lips, gaging the chap.

We Return Sparkling

Spun   this tendency to whirl, tendency to fall
gossamer. Thread what must pull back: my muscle mimics
your muscle gorges energy & *loves nothing, loves nothing.*
Axis of spine, gravity possesses   imprints
brief on lungs, vocal cords, belly: a charcoal sketch
against the light   silhouette wipes
in the turn.   We burn out of burn   & skin another universe
encases this   headache inching outside the head.
Our once watery lungs   the revolving lure of sea
brine in our nails, ocean of aortic sack—feel us beating: waves.
A sky is a sky is blue veins. We return   sparkling
& out of breath   tethered to gorgeous rules.

Across the Blown, Inward Breeze

The thicket of mind spreads
for wild reaps wild. The moon casting

light from other—how embrace
lends to give. See here, the glow

enters the pupils and now we are triune.
Another pedal unfurls in the thicket. Wild

sow. Wild reap. In the blink, we absorb
the night hungry and unfaithful. Breeze

feathers us. We lull in cricket wings, pastures
in other skulls, where the cool comes from.

Echo of leaf chatter does not dream
of us. Still not—

your chatter bones, your chatter
pumps of veins. Only in rhythms

do we know the crooks, bedded
earth—a stream

we trace an ear lobe, longing
for drum: rabbit hole, badger scent,

woodpecker's knot: tendril of brain
we carve out of. Self has never been
a singular thing to brand our own.

Toward the End of Day

To the left of the yard, a dog bellows beyond, unseen;
to the right, a siren leaves a garage from down the street.
Somewhere in the middle: small voices, skateboard wheels
on pavement, the lack of a marching band dictates the season,
& the empty whoosh of where traffic once was. Always this
in between. In this space, I watch the shadow of the Elm
tree swallow the shadow of the fence. Intersections
gobble & then...otherness. The sun ignores me; always looping
west—funny thing about orbs: the spin the spin & direction
eats you up from the inside out. Reminds me of the song Chris
left playing for me in a loop, over and over for my birthday:
*Your older than you've ever been & now your even older. & now
your even older. & now your even older.* We don't really loop though
do we? The dandelion sprouts & decays in the same plot; the lot
of life we tend, tends us. This fixation/asphyxiation with walls
& windows & property lines & the iron candelabra swinging
in the breeze even when I'm not around to witness, keeps me
tethered; render me a dandelion-picked, just as my roots gray
& I am all transparent film, I pray a contemplative child swoop
me out of my burrowing body, kiss me with her breath, & spread
this last moment of limb & heart & frontal lobe synapsing
into the wake of sun's tumble from the heavens; even in all
its glorious ignorance of my ride, I ride simple & badged in wind.

Hummingbirds

And the purple begonias bloom
on the vine, hug the parking sign—old friends.
Cacophony of colors draws this scene
outside my head attention gathers.

I walk through the cloud of gnats, wanting
to open my eyes, wanting to stay present
in the swarm. This piecemeal life
illuminates in a simple stroll. *Humming-*

birds ate my tomatoes, she whispers between our bodies
running her delicate fingers over a bike tire
on the sidewalk we lack no distance. Her smile
bunches at the edges of her mouth, I'm found

here in the soft breeze, burnt oranges and golden
leaves anoint my head. A swell in my throat
turns my head from hers. My chest a buzz:
a tiny heart beating with gale force. A gust

spools the lovely dust—her hair caught
a wisp of fall, of season, longing back; her
small gait, leading me along the row of trees; she
always displaying flight; always she lightly dancing in;

deep swallow in absence; and with wings
in dizzying momentum, she floats and floats and floats.

Soon

{otherwise known as moment of anointment}

& pods whirl off the cottonwood; mimic
hail in a gale of foliage. *The weight of you,*

cranium & aortic valve, in rhythm of
what the tree desires. Spring erupts

in tips of aspen branches: buds toss
their cracked & drying casings: a rain

of seasons—*discards* on my shoulder
baptize me in the name of

irreverence of the world's fall from winter.
Here, too, in the wake of *shed.* This cycle

predicate & foreign bodied I crawl from I
wounded & suckling: a sprig undulating

at root. *What of this divining rod?* My toes
burrow in soil; my hairs stand to greet

sun burnt & wheeling mother. Distance
wraps in sorrow when her tower-embrace

lulls in chills of ice & shallow days. Sun,
she weaves, unknowing, this divinity of

tilt. I stand barefoot in a patch of green
among the tired & wilted ground, cheek

& chin astute to the sky: *feel her spin;*
a large spider in the barn of your bones. I am

mortise, carved, in wait of tenon. Ribs
arc in orbit of body: design

tethers in open palms & eyelids bare
deepest red, in constant tilt, in promise: *soon.*

Blue Jays in the Yard

Beyond the pane: dark suspends and a forlorn look
crosses the day's face. Beyond the pane: two blue jays
pop from the belly of the lilac bush. Backs cerulean
flowing cobalt, flowing aquamarine—
limitless colors
bleed in feathers dipped gently in white, sculpted
patterns of tiles on southwest rooftops, back-drop
against the late fall greens of the yard—spell
bind this watcher, this gatherer of moments.
My hips push the desk forward; palms to the sill.
What playful seeking
close, closer to these walls? Proximity tugs
my ribs and knee caps react without my permission.
A rhythm in my chest panics my breath; *missing,*
yes missing. Led to the back door, I witness
what this gather lets me witness—small
steps, head slights, swivels, swivels. Reflection
in the glass and arms unlock the sliding door. Wings
expand and disrupt the mournful season. *Flashes.*
Flashes of indigo spiral
in the full dilation of pupils wanting, *wanting.*

Acknowledgments

Grateful acknowledgment to Jon Thompson for selecting my manuscript for Free Verse Editions at Parlor Press, and to David Blakesley for his design and attention to these pages.

Thank you to Kristy Bowen, editor of Dancing Girl Press, for selecting the entire poem "Imbibe {et alia} here" for publication as a chapbook released in 2016.

Profound gratitude to the journals and editors in which these poems first appeared, as well as the teams of individuals who create magic with hours of layouts and edits to bring creative writing, and specifically poetry, to life. Thank you.

ellipsis...journal of literature and art, "In bright"; *Dogwood: A Journal of Poetry & Prose,* sections [Cast {in/away} of—], [Bribe the whalebone in your back—], [What lends to the transit:], [Slur "and per se" —], [More than twice-removed], [We watch, through sorrow and lenses], [The wheelbarrows all], [Autonomic {all], [Leave this distance; this observation], and [Once the empty heavies] from "Imbibe {et alia} here"; *North American Review,* "A Long Road Never Takes Us"; *Poetrybay,* "Across the blown, inward breeze"; *Potomac Review,* "We return sparkling"; *Tarpaulin Sky Magazine,* "In Perihelion", "Broken Things" and "Centripetal"; *The Adirondack Review,* "Toward the End of Day"; *The Carolina Quarterly,* "{Honest} Random {Caused By Desire to De-Categorize} Self"; *The Normal School (Online),* "Alone at the lake", "In hush", and "Picture of the Hive"; *The Pinch Journal,* "Before Winter"; *Witness Magazine,* sections [These bones in the mouth], [Truant, your idle], [When cupped, the hand], [What interiors the egg], [On the topic of legerdemain], and [No, the hive sags] from "Imbibe {et alia} here".

A huge thanks to Jessica Owings Crouch for her magnificent artwork, *Flurry of Wings: Clustered,* for the cover of this book.

This book developed with the support and love of my family, friends, mentors, and teachers. Special thanks to Mel, Joe, and Mom who continue to encourage me to fully live my dreams, to be the person and poet I want to be. To Stephanie G'Schwind and John Calder-azzo, who through their huge hearts find unexpected ways to give to my poetic life. To Dan Beachy-Quick for showing me doors. To Foula Dimopoulos for being my friend when most needed; loves to you, friend.

To Chris, how you read these poems, hold my hand, wipe my tears with your palms, pucker your lips to make me laugh (as that's where your power derives), and how you un-waiver in your belief of me. Truly, I marvel at this life we share. I am thankful, to the core, for you. I love you.

Finally, to readers of poetry and those who have spent time in these pages, thank you, thank you. You keep poetry alive.

Free Verse Editions

Edited by Jon Thompson

13 ways of happily by Emily Carr
& in Open, Marvel by Felicia Zamora
Between the Twilight and the Sky by Jennie Neighbors
Blood Orbits by Ger Killeen
The Bodies by Chris Sindt
The Book of Isaac by Aidan Semmens
Canticle of the Night Path by Jennifer Atkinson
Child in the Road by Cindy Savett
Condominium of the Flesh by Valerio Magrelli, trans. by Clarissa Botsford
Contrapuntal by Christopher Kondrich
Country Album by James Capozzi
The Curiosities by Brittany Perham
Current by Lisa Fishman
Day In, Day Out by Simon Smith
Dear Reader by Bruce Bond
Dismantling the Angel by Eric Pankey
Divination Machine by F. Daniel Rzicznek
Erros by Morgan Lucas Schuldt
Fifteen Seconds without Sorrow by Shim Bo-Seon, translated by Chung
     Eun-Gwi and Brother Anthony of Taizé
The Forever Notes by Ethel Rackin
The Flying House by Dawn-Michelle Baude
Go On by Ethel Rackin
Instances: Selected Poems by Jeongrye Choi, translated by Brenda Hillman,
     Wayne de Fremery, & Jeongrye Choi
The Magnetic Brackets by Jesús Losada, translated by Michael Smith &
     Luis Ingelmo
Man Praying by Donald Platt
A Map of Faring by Peter Riley
The Miraculous Courageous by Josh Booton
No Shape Bends the River So Long by Monica Berlin & Beth Marzoni
Overyellow, by Nicolas Pesquès, translated by Cole Swensen
Physis by Nicolas Pesque, translated by Cole Swensen
Pilgrimage Suites by Derek Gromadzki
Pilgrimly by Siobhán Scarry
Poems from above the Hill & Selected Work by Ashur Etwebi, translated by
     Brenda Hillman & Diallah Haidar

The Prison Poems by Miguel Hernández, translated by Michael Smith
Puppet Wardrobe by Daniel Tiffany
Quarry by Carolyn Guinzio
remanence by Boyer Rickel
Rumor by Elizabeth Robinson
Signs Following by Ger Killeen
Split the Crow by Sarah Sousa
Spine by Carolyn Guinzio
Spool by Matthew Cooperman
Summoned by Guillevic, translated by Monique Chefdor & Stella Harvey
Sunshine Wound by L. S. Klatt
System and Population, by Christopher Sindt
These Beautiful Limits by Thomas Lisk
They Who Saw the Deep by Geraldine Monk
The Thinking Eye by Jennifer Atkinson
This History That Just Happened by Hannah Craig
An Unchanging Blue: Selected Poems 1962–1975 by Rolf Dieter
    Brinkmann, translated by Mark Terrill
Under the Quick by Molly Bendall
Verge by Morgan Lucas Schuldt
The Wash by Adam Clay
We'll See by Georges Godeau, translated by Kathleen McGookey
What Stillness Illuminated by Yermiyahu Ahron Taub
Winter Journey [Viaggio d'inverno] by Attilio Bertolucci, translated by
    Nicholas Benson
Wonder Rooms by Allison Funk

About the Author

Felicia Zamora is the author of the books *Of Form & Gather*, winner of the 2016 Andrés Montoya Poetry Prize (University of Notre Dame Press) and *Instrument of Gaps* (forthcoming from Slope Editions 2017). *Of Form & Gather* was listed as one of the "9 Outstanding Latino Books Recently Published by Independent and University Presses" by NBC News. She won the 2015 Tomaž Šalamun Prize from *Verse*, and authored two chapbooks. Her published works may be found or forthcoming in *Alaska Quarterly Review, Beloit Poetry Review, Columbia Poetry Review, Crazyhorse, Hotel Amerika, Indiana Review, jubilat, Meridian, Notre Dame Review, North American Review, OmniVerse, Pleiades, Poetry Daily, Poetry Northwest, Prairie Schooner, Puerto del Sol, Sugar House Review, Tarpaulin Sky Magazine, The Adirondack Review, The Cincinnati Review, The Georgia Review, The Michigan Quarterly, TriQuarterly Review, Tupelo Quarterly, Verse Daily, Witness Magazine, West Branch*, and others. She is an associate poetry editor for the *Colorado Review* and holds an MFA from Colorado State University. She is the 2017 Poet Laureate for Fort Collins, Colorado, and education programs coordinator for the Virginia G. Piper Center for Creative Writing at Arizona State University. She lives in Phoenix, Arizona, with her partner Chris and their two dogs.

Photograph of the author by Chris Van Wyk.
Used by permission.

CPSIA information can be obtained
at www.ICGtesting.com
Printed in the USA
FSOW01n0255231017
40152FS